JOHN BETJEMAN

JOHN
BETJEMAN

by
JOHN PRESS

Edited by Ian Scott-Kilvert

PUBLISHED FOR
THE BRITISH COUNCIL
BY LONGMAN GROUP LTD

LONGMAN GROUP LTD
Longman House, Burnt Mill, Harlow, Essex

*Associated companies, branches and
representatives throughout the world*

First published 1974
© John Press 1974

*Printed in Great Britain by
Headley Brothers Limited, London and Ashford, Kent*

ISBN 0 582 01239 2

CONTENTS

I. INTRODUCTION

JOHN Sparrow's Preface to John Betjeman's *Selected Poems* (1948) reminds us that at one time Betjeman was in danger of becoming an eccentric, modish poet, admired only by a little circle of devotees who took a sophisticated pleasure in the cult of Victoriana which had sprung up in the Oxford of the 1920s:

It looked indeed as if Mr Betjeman was fated to end his days as the Laureate of the suburbs and the Gothic Revival.

Today Sir John (he was knighted in 1969) is more widely known than any other living English poet. His appointment to the Laureateship in 1972 was acclaimed by millions of people who probably scarcely knew the name and had never read a page of any other contemporary poet. This was partly because he had by then become a popular figure on television, where his prowess on TV panels and his programmes on architecture and topography had won him an enormous audience. The first edition of his *Collected Poems* (1958) reputedly sold more than a hundred thousand copies, and enjoyed a success unparalleled since his publishers brought out Byron's *Don Juan* in Regency England. He is a friend of the Royal Family and a pillar of what may be loosely called the literary and artistic Establishment, a Companion of Literature, a former Royal Fine Art Commissioner, a holder of honorary doctorates from several universities. Despite the jealousies and feuds of the literary world, the majority of his fellow poets welcomed his succession to the Laureateship. Like one of his most illustrious predecessors, Lord Tennyson, he appeals to a very wide public, and manages to voice the aspirations of many ordinary people, while retaining the respect of his fellow practitioners, even if some of them are a little scornful of his showmanship and a trifle weary of reading about his teddy bear Archibald, which fulfils much the same role as Winston Churchill's cigars.

It is clear that Betjeman is an extraordinary character who has, over the years since he first delighted his friends at Oxford, enjoyed a remarkable career. Although it is not easy to disentangle the achievement of the artist from the trappings of his personality, the purpose of this essay is to trace his progress as a writer in prose and in verse and to illustrate the range and variety of his work.

II. LIFE

John Betjeman, who was born in 1906, was the only child of Ernest Betjeman, the head of a prosperous family business which made furnishings and other domestic objects for expensive shops. We can reconstruct Betjeman's early life not only from his autobiography in verse, *Summoned by Bells* (1960), but from a score of short poems which refer to incidents of his childhood. Those who believe that the first few years of our lives determine our natures and our destinies can find in Betjeman's poems a wealth of material to support their thesis. We learn of his love for his parents, his gentle, devout mother, and his stone-deaf father, with whom his relations were later to become strained. Betjeman soon learned to distinguish the subtle, deadly gradations of class, hierarchy and snobbery which animated the quietly opulent North-London Edwardian suburbs in which he was bred. He caught the ineradicable terror of death and of damnation from a Calvinist nursery maid. Perhaps his most poignant evocation of his childhood world is to be found in these stanzas from 'St Saviour's, Aberdeen Park, Highbury, London, N':

These were the streets my parents knew when they loved and
won—
The brougham that crunched the gravel, the laurel-girt
paths that wind,
Geranium-beds for the lawn, Venetian blinds for the sun,
A separate tradesman's entrance, straw in the mews behind,
Just in the four-mile radius where hackney carriages run,
Solid Italianate houses for the solid commercial mind.

These were the streets they knew; and I, by descent, belong
To these tall neglected houses divided into flats.
Only the church remains, where carriages used to throng
And my mother stepped out in flounces and my father
stepped out in spats

To shadowy stained-glass matins or gas-lit evensong
   And back in a country quiet with doffing of chimney hats.

Great red church of my parents, cruciform crossing they
                               knew—
   Over these same encaustics they and their parents trod
Bound through a red-brick transept for a once familiar pew
   Where the organ set them singing and the sermon let them
                               nod
And up this coloured brickwork the same long shadows grew
   As these in the stencilled chancel where I kneel in the
                         presence of God.

From an early age Betjeman longed to be a poet. At his preparatory school in Highgate one of the masters was T. S. Eliot. Betjeman had already written a great many poems and believed that they were as good as those of the early-nineteenth-century poet Thomas Campbell:

> And so I bound my verse into a book,
> *The Best of Betjeman*, and handed it
> To one who, I was told, liked poetry—
> The American master, Mr Eliot.

His adolescent years were darkened by his unhappiness at his public school, Marlborough, where vicious bullying was rampant. One of the masters, H. L. O. Flecker, a brother of the poet James Elroy Flecker, read aloud and mocked a poem on a city church written by Betjeman when he was fifteen, an incident which left Betjeman with a lifelong hatred and fear of destructive criticism. He was also made unhappy by the deterioration of his relationship with his father, who wished to be taken for a country gentleman, and who tried in vain to instil into his son his own enthusiasm for shooting and fishing.

Oxford was a delight after Marlborough. Maurice Bowra, later Warden of Wadham and at that time a young don, tells us in his *Memories* (1966) that he immediately recognized the originality of Betjeman's mind, and his extraordinary familiarity with the bypaths of the Victorian age. He also admired such poems as 'Death in Leamington', 'The Arrest of Oscar Wilde at the Cadogan Hotel' and 'Hymn'. Betjeman ran up large bills for expensive architectural books which he hoped his father would pay, mixed with under-graduates who provided material for the early novels of Evelyn Waugh, and neglected the work which he should have been doing for his degree in English. His tutor, C. S. Lewis, ignorant or contemptuous of Betjeman's genuine learning in his own chosen fields, had little sympathy with his literary aspirations. When Betjeman, after more than one attempt, failed to pass a ludicrously easy qualifying examination called Divinity Moderations, he was obliged to leave Oxford without taking his Finals. C. S. Lewis dourly remarked 'You'd have only got a Third,' but to Betjeman exile from Oxford was a blow:

> I'd seen myself a don,
> Reading old poets in the library
> Attending chapel in an M.A. gown
> And sipping vintage port by candlelight.

Most of his references to Oxford are affectionate, but the portraits of dons in *An Oxford University Chest* (1938) are sharply satirical, and 'May Day Song for North Oxford' contains an ironical allusion to his old tutor:

> Oh! well-bound Wells and Bridges! Oh! earnest ethical
> search
> For the wide high-table λογος of St C. S. Lewis's Church.

Betjeman also makes a slightly barbed comment in the Acknowledgements to his Shell Guide, *Devon* (1936):

For mental inspiration the Editor had only to think of Mr C. S. LEWIS, tweed-clad and jolly, to get busy with his pen.

After a hilarious episode, again reminiscent of Evelyn Waugh, in which Betjeman got a job at a school by pre-tending to be a devotee of cricket, he obtained a post on *The Architectural Review*, thanks to the influence of Maurice Bowra. The salary was £300 a year, which Betjeman regarded as a pittance, although it compared favourably with the salaries of young professional men at that period. In 1933 he married Penelope, daughter of Field-Marshal Sir Philip (later Lord) Chetwode, Commander-in-Chief, India. According to Bowra, Lady Chetwode produced a remark worthy of Wilde's Lady Bracknell when, in the early days of

Betjeman's friendship with her daughter, she said 'We ask people like that to our houses, but we don't marry them'.

Despite his father's pleas and his own sense of guilt at his failure to carry on the family business, Betjeman continued to live by his pen. During the Second World War he worked for a time as United Kingdom Press Attaché in Dublin, and served also in the Admiralty and in the Books Department of the British Council, which was then housed in temporary hutments in Blenheim Palace, near Oxford. After the war he resumed his career as a journalist and, as the influence of television increased, became one of the most accomplished masters of the new medium. The growth of his fame as a TV performer accompanied his rise in a more august world. A guest at Windsor Castle, a Commander of the British Empire, a Governor of the Oxford Anglican study centre, Pusey House, Betjeman is more warmly admired by the Court, by fashionable society and by academics than any Laureate since Tennyson.

Yet, despite his renown as a public entertainer and the presence of autobiographical elements in his writings, Betjeman has contrived to remain a private figure, the very opposite of the confessional writer who bares his inner life to the public gaze. His loyalty to old friends and his kindness and generosity to the humble and obscure are, like his family life, largely unknown and unpublicized. Instead of lingering any longer on biographical details, we should now turn to consider the prose writings which stretch from *Ghastly Good Taste* (1933) to *West Country Churches* (1973).

III. PROSE WORKS

Anybody who has seen Betjeman on the television screen can hardly fail to be enchanted, whether he is discoursing on Baronial Gothic in Australia, an English country house, or the Metropolitan Railway. He communicates to his audience a wealth of fascinating information with no trace of pedantry or condescension. His zest, exuberance and gaiety are irresistible. Tom Driberg's article 'A Walk with Mr Betjeman', which appeared in the *New Statesman*, 6 January 1961,

2•

conveys something of the quality of Betjeman's conversation. Betjeman took Driberg on a brief tour of the City of London on foot—'As you haven't brought a bicycle we shall have to walk'—and proceeded to pour out a stream of lively and perceptive comments on the buildings old and new which passed before their eyes. Betjeman's marvellous knowledge of London's social and architectural history continually illuminated the view of the churches, monuments, shops and public buildings. He rejoiced in Blackfriars Station, one of whose façades is adorned with heavily rusticated pilasters, into which are cut the names of the principal stations once served by the South Eastern and Chatham Railway: Beckenham and Baden-Baden, Walmer and Wiesbaden, Westgate-on-Sea and St Petersburg. 'Mr Betjeman', so Driberg assures us, 'once went in and asked for a ticket to St Petersburg: the clerk referred him to Victoria (Continental) without a flicker of surprise.'

Even on the printed page the ease and warmth of Betjeman's conversational style carry the reader along, holding his attention from start to finish, giving him a sense of listening to an intimate, friendly voice talking in a relaxed tone. Betjeman's prose works are almost all topographical essays, or guides to certain aspects of English architecture. It would be unrewarding to attempt a summary of these works, especially as they advance no formal thesis and put forward no systematic aesthetic doctrine. Betjeman is not primarily an art historian, nor does he pretend to be a detached observer, recording in a tone of dry neutrality the evolution of architecture in these islands. He is a partisan, passionately involved in his theme, celebrating what he loves, excoriating what he detests. It is significant that the title of his most substantial book should be *First and Last Loves* (1952).

It may be useful to trace briefly the growth of his aesthetic taste, and to indicate the values which have guided his writing on architecture over the last forty years. The second edition of *Ghastly Good Taste*, which appeared in 1970, contains an introduction by the author entitled 'An Aesthetic Apologia', the story of Betjeman's intellectual and artistic development from boyhood to the eve of his marriage in

1933. Even before going to Marlborough Betjeman had developed a voracious, undiscriminating appetite for old buildings, particularly for anything which was, or purported to be, medieval or Tudor. At Marlborough he learned to love eighteenth-century buildings and Victorian art and poetry, although at this stage he did not take seriously Victorian architecture, and before going up to Oxford he had come to dislike Gothic. During his time at Oxford he was invited to stay at a number of Irish eighteenth-century houses, an experience which led him to believe that Ireland was the most beautiful country in the world, and gave him a lasting admiration for the virtues of the Anglo-Irish ruling classes. Another factor which permanently influenced his taste was his reading of A. E. Richardson's *Monumental Classic Architecture in Great Britain and Ireland* (1914).

During the General Strike of 1926 he tried to help the strikers, waiting in vain at Didcot to carry messages for the National Union of Railwaymen. He was at this period a parlour pink, a follower of Conrad Noel, the 'Red Vicar' of Thaxted in Essex, who wanted to restore medieval joy and simplicity to the lives of twentieth-century men and women. His employment on *The Architectural Review* brought him into contact with elderly architects, survivors of the Victorian and the Edwardian eras, as well as with the apostles of modernism. Since then his study of architecture has become more exact and profound; his love of Gothic has strengthened; his knowledge of Victorian architecture has grown more extensive and more discriminating. The body of his work testifies to his familiarity with countless villages, small towns, ports, churches, railway stations, public houses, theatres, canals, gardens, bridges, barns, shops, petrol stations and street lamps in every part of the country.

It is a more complex task to summarize the artistic and spiritual principles which have informed his essays and other architectural writings since the early 1930s. Popular and superficial accounts of Betjeman portray him as an idolater of the past, with a special fondness for Victorian buildings even when they are third-rate; as a compulsive protester who leaps into action whenever any kind of ancient relic is threatened with destruction. It is alleged that he is out of touch with the realities of contemporary life; that he takes little interest in the housing of the masses; that his attacks on bureaucracy are vitiated by his failure to understand the necessity of large-scale governmental planning in town and countryside. He is, on this view, a romantic individualist steeped in nostalgia for the hierarchical society of earlier ages, a sophisticated modern version of a Victorian aesthete.

Such a portrait of Betjeman is a mere caricature. His favourite architectural period is not the Victorian age but the first quarter of the nineteenth century. Nor does he praise indiscriminately the work of Victorian architects and the vanished streets of London. In *Victorian and Edwardian London from Old Photographs* (1969) he describes a photograph of Hampstead Road taken in 1904:

When I look at the noisy muddle . . . as depicted in the photograph and see the faceless efficiency of overpass and underpass churning in its clouds of diesel through the impersonal slabs which are there now, I realize we have only changed one sort of bad for another sort of bad.

It is untrue that he cares little for the needs of ordinary people in a modern industrial society. He remarks in *English Cities and Small Towns* (1943) that 'to someone who likes people as well as buildings, the industrial towns are the hope and life of England'. In the same essay he declares that 'only by planning on a national scale will we preserve the hundreds of beautiful old cities of England', although he goes on to warn his readers that 'a single year of over-enthusiastic "post-war reconstruction" may destroy the lot'. As long ago as 1937, in *Antiquarian Prejudice*, a pamphlet reprinted in *First and Last Loves*, he was arguing in favour of well-planned prefabricated houses:

I see no hope for the majority until they are made here. Lord Nuffield had a wonderful opportunity to make them at his pressed-steel works at Oxford. He missed it, and many of his workers are housed in some of the worst speculative estates to be seen.

It is this same concern for the quality of human life which has recently led him to denounce the proposal to drive motorways through various residential districts of London.

Betjeman has always responded to architecture as the visible manifestation of the spiritual life of a society. When, in *Vintage London* (1942), he laments the passing of old London it is the inhabitants of that vanished city whom he celebrates. Every year, he says, old London lessens,

as more and more of its members are carried with all the pomp of a long subscription to the Burial Society to that most Victorian sight of all London—the windy Carrara-covered cemetery.

He observes elsewhere that a modern crematorium is the appropriate resting place for those who spend so many hours in an Odeon cinema. Architecture is for him the reflection not only of a society's political and economic structure but an outward and visible sign of an inward and spiritual grace, or lack of grace. Or, as Francis Thompson wrote:

> Our towns are copied fragments from our breast:
> And all man's Babylons strive but to impart
> The grandeurs of his Babylonian heart.

Betjeman's approach to the visual arts is diametrically opposed to that of Roger Fry, who remarked in a letter written in 1920: 'It's all the same to me if I represent a Christ or a saucepan, since it's the form and not the object itself that interests me.' Betjeman wants to preserve old buildings for a variety of reasons, but mainly because of their human associations, which are indeed inseparable from their aesthetic power and beauty. He would echo an observation made by Thomas Hardy in a paper which he prepared in 1906 to be read before the Society for the Protection of Ancient Buildings:

I think that the damage done to the sentiment of association by replacement, by the rupture of continuity, is mainly why our loss is so tragic. To protect a building against renewal in fresh materials is more of a social—I may say a humane—duty than an aesthetic one.

It is clear from a study of his work that, in his writings about architecture, Betjeman is almost invariably a passionate advocate of certain moral and cultural values. The opening paragraph of *Antiquarian Prejudice*, originally delivered as a lecture to the Group Theatre, succinctly conveys the spirit of his entire work in this field:

I come to you fresh from Evensong and with my outlook widened. Architecture has a wider meaning than that which is commonly given to it. For architecture means not a house, or a single building or a church, or Sir Herbert Baker, or the glass at Chartres, but your surroundings, not a town or a street, but our whole over-populated island. It is concerned with where we eat, work, sleep, play, congregate, escape. It is our background, alas, often too permanent.

He has unceasingly attacked those speculators and bureaucrats whose rapacity and unimaginative insensibility have devastated Britain more wantonly and irreparably than the raids of the Nazi bombers. In *Vintage London*, he observes that 'Non-vintage London of to-day extends over most of Britain', and places the blame squarely where it belongs:

The speculative builder is abetted by the contractor, who is abetted by the Building Society, which is abetted by the Banks; and these sinister agents have their central organisations in London.

Betjeman's loathing for the speculative builder is fierce enough to satisfy the most ardent Marxist. Indeed he detests our society for its worship of money. The prefatory essay in his collection of architectural essays, *First and Last Loves*, denounces the perverted values by which we live:

We accept the collapse of the fabrics of our old churches, the thieving of lead and objects from them, the commandeering and butchery of our scenery by the services, the despoiling of landscaped parks and the abandonment to a fate worse than the workhouse of our country houses, because we are convinced we must save money.

Nor does he spare bureaucrats, civil or ecclesiastical, who advance good reasons for allying themselves with the vandals. He describes in *The Spectator*[1] the incivility he encountered at the hands of the Town Clerk of Fulham when he went to inspect The Grange, an old building threatened with destruction, and he waxes satirical over an

[1] Issues of 16 July and 27 August 1954.

14

Archdeacon who referred to a splendid old church as a heavy drain on the financial resources of the diocese, and indicates his low view of the Anglican hierarchy:

Bishops are becoming the slaves of finance. They do not realise that a beautiful church is a more lasting witness to the Faith than they are.

We are witnessing, says Betjeman, the apotheosis of suburban man, whose yearning for culture is little more than an expression of restlessness and no more fruitful than the proliferation of government housing schemes:

By looking only at well-laid-out municipal estates and averting one's eyes from the acres of unimaginative modern housing, by forgetting those terrible pipe-dreams come true of thicknecked brutes with flashy cars, elderly blondes and television sets—those modernistic, Egyptian, beaux-arts and other façades of the new factories outside every large town, by ignoring all these and much more, it is possible to live in a fool's paradise of imagined culture, a sort of Welwyn Garden City of the mind.

No wonder that he calls this prefatory essay 'Love is Dead' and quotes the Collect for Quinquagesima from the Book of Common Prayer, thus linking the restoration of artistic health with the gift of love:

O Lord, who hast taught us that all our doings without charity are nothing worth; Send thy Holy Ghost, and pour into our hearts that most excellent gift of charity, the very bond of peace and of all virtues, without which whosoever liveth is counted dead before thee. Grant this for thine only Son Jesus Christ's sake.

Betjeman writes admirable prose, which is always beguilingly readable, and which at times commands an effective polemical force. His range is wide: he can describe with mocking and merciless accuracy a landscape devastated by greed and insensitivity; he can portray with a wealth of loving detail a vanished way of life; he can evoke the harmonious pattern of the English countryside where man has enriched the bounty of nature; he can bring before our eyes the architectural richness and uniqueness of our cathedrals. Two passages of some length may convey something of Betjeman's gifts as a prose writer. The first, taken from his Rede Lecture at Cambridge, *The English Town in the last Hundred Years* (1956), is a good example of Betjeman's powers of persuasion, his ability to describe with deadly precision the spoliation of the countryside by ignorance, misguided progressiveness, greed and the unchecked ravages of technology:

Those old thatched cottages of the water colours have been condemned by Medical Officers of Health, who know as much about architecture as I know about whooping cough. These cottages have been destroyed instead of enlarged and modernized, as they could have been for less than the cost of a new council house, because people who do not care for what is old sincerely believe that only what is new is worth having. In the old farm buildings, the fine barns have been replaced by Dutch barns or patched with concrete and sheets of corrugated iron. Hedges are fast disappearing and giving way to concrete posts supporting chain-link fencing. Elms have been felled for fear one of their branches will fall on a ratepayer, and no trees have been planted in their stead. Where the village smithy stood is now a garage with a front like a modernistic chimney-piece magnified forty times and the tin signs set out along the road for a hundred yards in either direction. Poles and wires are everywhere: Post Office wires on one side of the road, the thicker wires of the Central Electricity Board on the other; and a transformer like a monkey up a stick is given the most prominent skyline in sight in the village.

The second passage, from *Collins Guide to English Parish Churches* (1958), reveals Betjeman in a quieter, more appreciative vein, although the gentleness of tone is reinforced by a few tartly satirical observations. He is celebrating with a glowing but unsentimental romanticism the diverse character of the parish churches which he knows so intimately and loves so much:

The Parish Churches of England are even more varied than the landscape. The tall town church, smelling of furniture polish and hot-water pipes, a shadow of the medieval marvel it once was, so assiduously have Victorian and even later restorers renewed everything old; the little weather-beaten hamlet church standing in a farmyard down a narrow lane, bat-droppings over the pews and one service a month; the church of a once prosperous village, a relic of the 15th-century wool trade, whose soaring splen-

dour of stone and glass subsequent generations have had neither
the energy nor the money to destroy; the suburban church
with Northamptonshire-style steeple rising unexpectedly above
slate roofs of London and calling with mid-Victorian bells to
the ghosts of merchant carriage folk for whom it was built; the
tin chapel-of-ease on the edge of the industrial estate; the High,
the Low, the Central churches, the alive and the dead ones, the
churches that are easy to pray in and those that are not, the churches
whose architecture brings you to your knees, the churches whose
decorations affront the sight—all these come within the wide
embrace of our Anglican Church, whose arms extend beyond
the seas to many fabrics more.

Although he is never pedantic or over-solemn, Betjeman
is a consistently serious writer, whose books and essays on
architecture display firm moral and social principles no less
than a penetrating and highly individual aesthetic percep-
tiveness. He may have taken a youthful pleasure in affronting
the duller Oxford dons by praising the more hideous
examples of Victorian *objets d'art*, but he soon developed a
mature understanding and love of Victorian architecture
and did much to open our eyes to its merits. His writings
are less weighty and scholarly than the major works of
Kenneth Clark, John Summerson and H. S. Goodhart-
Rendel, to name only three architectural historians whom
Betjeman himself praises for their labours as pioneers in the
appreciation of Victorian building. Nevertheless, he has
probably done more than any other single person to bring
about the decisive change in our attitude to the Victorian
achievement in the visual arts.

Nor is he merely one of those figures who acquire a
modish reputation by influencing the taste of the day. He is
in the direct line of descent from such Victorian sages as
Ruskin and Morris, whose love of the arts was linked with
their desire for the regeneration of society. Betjeman lacks
Morris's prophetic vision of a world in which men live as
brothers, just as he seldom attains the magnificence of
Ruskin's finest prose, Yet, in a more modest and wittier
spirit, he has fought the same battles. 'We must lift [people's]
eyes from the privet hedge to the hills', he declares in his
Rede Lecture, and he goes on to say that 'for the . . . impor-

17

tant missionary work of opening people's eyes we have the film and television'. As long ago as 1933 he expressed certain fundamental beliefs about architecture and society, in the final paragraph of *Ghastly Good Taste:*

Architecture can only be made alive again by a new order and another Christendom. I repeat that I do not know what form that Christendom will take, for I am not an economist. It is unlikely it will be capitalism. Whatever it is, this generation will not see it.

The whole body of his prose is animated by his desire to further the coming of that Christendom.

IV. POETRY: THEMES AND CHARACTER

Although Betjeman's prose writings are more substantial than is often supposed he is first and foremost a poet. While his books and essays have expressed strongly-held convictions, and even his gifts as a public entertainer have been employed to open people's eyes to their surroundings, Betjeman has said that his prose has been 'primarily a means of earning money in order to buy the free time in which to write poetry'. He may, in ironical self-deprecation, have referred to himself as 'the Ella Wheeler Wilcox *de nos jours*', but his sense of vocation has always been strong. His declaration in *Summoned by Bells* rings true:

> For myself,
> I knew as soon as I could read and write
> That I must be a poet. Even today,
> When all the way from Cambridge[1] comes a wind
> To blow the lamps out every time they're lit,
> I know that I must light mine up again.

It is a mark of his originality and authenticity as a poet that he has always remained indifferent to changes in poetic fashion and to dominant critical shibboleths. Just as he ignored the doctrines of Roger Fry in the field of the visual arts, so he remained unaffected by the modernist movement in poetry, which was all the rage in his undergraduate days.

[1] Referring to a school of criticism there, considered by many to be over-censorious.

The heritage of Symbolism, the revolution inaugurated by Yeats, Eliot and Pound, even the discovery of Hopkins, seem to have influenced him not at all. He resembles the mythical figure who prefers Dekker, Hawker and Flecker to Rilke, Kafka and Lorca. From the very start he has written unashamedly about the themes which evoke his love, his interest, his hatred and his amusement, and like Words-worth's true poet he has created the taste which now enjoys him.

His preface to *Old Lights for New Chancels* (1940) lists a few of the subjects which awaken in him the desire to compose a poem:

I love suburbs and gaslights and Pont Street and Gothic Revival churches and mineral railways, provincial towns and Garden cities.

Nor is he taking a perverse, mocking pleasure when he depicts scenes regarded by many as ugly, quaint or risible:

I see no harm in trying to describe overbuilt Surrey in verse. But when I do so I am not being satirical but topographical.

The part played by topography in Betjeman's poetry is so important that we must pause to consider its nature and significance. As an architectural historian, Betjeman delights in portraying with the utmost precision the minutest details of places and buildings, just as he relishes the subtlest inflex-ions of accents and modes of speech, and the intricate gradations of class and social hierarchies in English life. W. H. Auden's introduction to *Slick but not Streamlined* (1947), a selection of Betjeman's verse and prose, analyses what he calls *topophilia*:

Topophilia differs from the farmer's love of his home soil and the litterateur's fussy regional patriotism in that it is not possessive or limited to any one locality; the practised topophil can operate in a district he has never visited before. On the other hand, it has little in common with nature love. Wild or unhumanised nature holds no charms for the average topophil because it is lacking in history ... At the same time, though history mani-fested by objects is essential, the quality of the history and the quality of the object are irrelevant; a branch railroad is as valuable as a Roman wall, a neo-Tudor teashop as interesting as a Gothic cathedral.

Betjeman's love of landscape and in particular of the Cornish coast has become more apparent since Auden wrote these words, but in general this account of topophilia throws valuable light on Betjeman's poetry.

There is one aspect of Betjeman's topophilia and of his fondness for exact description which has not received much attention from his readers. We may approach it by considering certain qualities in the work of Tennyson, who is in many ways closer than any other poet to Betjeman. In a broadcast colloquium on Tennyson early in 1973 Betjeman referred to Tennyson as holding 'a very vague faith such as is mine'. Both poets find in the sea and in their childhood an immensely rich source of emotional power and resonance, and both are at times overwhelmed by an instinctive terror of death and a stifling horror aroused by the contemplation of eternity. Some of Betjeman's blank verse has a Tennysonian movement which may reflect more basic affinities. The following passage from Tennyson's *The Princess*, quoted by Betjeman in his 1940 Preface, clearly anticipates certain features of his descriptive verse:

> and on the pavement lay
> Carved stones of the Abbey-ruin in the park,
> Huge Ammonites, and the first bones of Time;
> And on the tables every clime and age
> Jumbled together; celts and calumets,
> Claymore and snowshoe, toys in lava, fans
> Of sandal, amber, ancient rosaries,
> Laborious orient ivy sphere in sphere,
> The cursed Malayan crease, and battle clubs
> From the isles of palm . . .

In his study of *Tennyson* (1972) Christopher Ricks follows Humphry House in conjecturing that Tennyson's minutely precise descriptions of external things stabilized his mind and allayed his restlessness. Ricks carries this speculation one stage further:

The same might be said of Tennyson's insistence upon accuracy in his poems (accuracy scientific, historical, reminiscential) . . . when [Harold] Nicolson speaks of Tennyson's 'maddening accuracy' it should be retorted that it may have maddened Nicolson but it helped to keep Tennyson sane.

It is probable that Betjeman's loving reconstruction of some historical incident and his concern for period detail spring from a similar emotional need.

At a time when most young poets were striving to emulate Hopkins or Eliot, John Betjeman was turning towards remote and unfashionable poetic sources. His 1940 Preface describes the kind of verse which has, from the beginning of his career, nourished his imagination:

> In the eighteenth century Dr Watts, Swift, Robert Lloyd, Thomson, Dyer, Shenstone, Mickle, Cowper and Burns are easily among my favourites, not for their finer flights, but for their topographical atmosphere. In the nineteenth century Crabbe, Praed, Hood, Clare, Ebenezer Elliott, Capt. Kennish, Neale, Tennyson, Charles Tennyson Turner, Clough, William Barnes, Meredith, William Morris and a score or so more. I find great pleasure in what is termed minor poetry, in long epics which never get into anthologies; topographical descriptions in verse published locally.

Compared with the enigmatic hints of Eliot, and the superb oracular revelations of Yeats about the creative process, Betjeman's account in *The Spectator*, 8 October 1954, of how he writes poems is unpretentiously straightforward:

> First there is the thrilling or terrifying recollection of a place, a person or a mood which hammers inside the head saying 'Go on! Go on! It is your duty to make a poem out of it'. Then a line or a phrase suggests itself. Next comes the selection of a metre. I am a traditionalist in metres and have made few experiments. The rhythms of Tennyson, Crabbe, Hawker, Dowson, Hardy, James Elroy Flecker, Moore and Hymns A & M[1] are generally buzzing about in my brain and I choose one from these which seems to me to suit the theme.

He jots down rough drafts on cigarette packets or old letters before writing them on foolscap, but the aural element remains dominant:

> Then I start reciting the lines aloud, either driving a car or on solitary walks, until the sound of the words satisfies me.

The names mentioned by Betjeman in the two passages quoted above by no means exhaust the poets who have

[1] *Hymns Ancient and Modern*, a widely used Anglican hymnbook.

influenced him. Reminiscences of Frederick Locker Lampson, Father Prout, Dibdin, William Allingham, Longfellow and Newbolt may be detected in his verse. The model for some of his poems is almost certainly Kipling, with whom he shares one or two basic attitudes: a robust patriotism; a mistrust of politicians, bureaucrats and progressive intellectuals; an extraordinary sensitiveness to pain and an understanding of loneliness fostered by experiences of bullying in childhood and youth which left a searing mark upon the tender skin; a fondness for controlled irony which sometimes bursts out into a scalding jet of fury. John Sparrow's review of his *Collected Poems* (1958) in *The Times Literary Supplement*, 12 December 1958, remarks on the affinities in tone and movement between Betjeman's verse and certain poems by John Meade Falkner, who is better known as a novelist than as a poet:

> *Post pugnam pausa fiet*;[1]
>> Lord, we have made our choice;
> In the stillness of autumn quiet,
>> We have heard the still, small voice.
> We have sung *Oh where shall Wisdom?*[2]
>> Thick paper, folio, Boyce.

And, from another poem:

> On the fly-leaves of these old prayer-books
>> The childish writings fade,
> Which show that once they were their books
>> In the days when prayer was made
> For other kings and princesses,
>> William and Adelaide . . .

> Is the almond-blossom bitter?
>> Is the grasshopper heavy to bear?
> Christ make me happier, fitter
>> To go to my own over there:
> Jerusalem the Golden,
>> What bliss beyond compare!

It is significant that Philip Larkin, one of Betjeman's most fervent admirers, has included in his *Oxford Book of*

---

[1] 'After the battle there shall be rest'.
[2] An anthem by William Boyce (1710-79).

Twentieth-Century English Verse (1973) the two poems, 'After Trinity' and 'Christmas', from which these extracts are respectively drawn.

It would be inappropriate in a brief essay to devote much space to the elements of parody, pastiche and allusion in Betjeman's poetry, and only a patient researcher endowed with an encyclopaedic knowledge of recondite poets of the eighteenth and nineteenth centuries could hope to track down all the references and echoes interwoven in the texture of Betjeman's verse. Yet this kind of device is so pervasive in his poetic *corpus* and affords such pleasure that we must glance for a moment at the way in which it operates.

Some poems are direct parodies of hymns or of famous Victorian poems. 'Dorset' is a smoothly elegant imitation of Hardy's 'Friends Beyond'; 'Love in a Valley' reproduces the metre, though not the spirit, of Meredith's 'Love in the Valley'; 'Huxley Hall' is based upon Tennyson's 'Locksley Hall' and is markedly inferior to its model. In many poems he is not so much imitating directly as fashioning a pastiche of minor poetry of the late nineteenth century. Or, to reverse the comparison, we may feel that a poem of that period appears to anticipate certain features of Betjeman's style. He himself, in *A Pictorial History of English Architecture* (1972), quotes, without revealing the source, a ballad on Bedford Park, a late-Victorian garden suburb built by Norman Shaw, one of Betjeman's favourite architects, The following stanza glitters and sparkles like a vintage Betjeman 1931:

> With red and blue and sagest green
>   Were walls and dado dyed,
> Friezes of Morris' there were seen
>   And oaken wainscot wide;
> Now he who loves aesthetic cheer
>   And does not mind the damp
> May come and read Rossetti here
>   By a Japanese-y lamp.

It is sometimes difficult to know whether Betjeman is deliberately borrowing, and relishing the pleasure of counterpointing one idiom against another, or whether he has so thoroughly absorbed an earlier poet's work into his own sensibility that no question of conscious imitation arises. John Sparrow says that we often enjoy Betjeman for his 'auditory associations, from hearing, as it were, a new song set to an old tune; sometimes the tune and pattern are his own as in "Wantage Bells".' He quotes a stanza from this poem:

> Wall flowers are bright in their beds
> And their scent all pervading,
> Withered are primroses' heads
> And the hyacinth fading
> But flowers by the score
> Multitudes more
> Weed flowers and seed flowers and mead flowers our
> > paths are invading.

A similar tune and pattern occur in a translation by Catherine Winkworth of a German hymn, which Betjeman may well have known, since it is to be found in *Hymns Ancient and Modern*:

> Praise to the Lord, the Almighty, the King of creation;
> O my soul praise him for he is thy health and salvation.
> All ye who hear,
> Now to His temple draw near,
> Joining in glad adoration.

Good poets have the power to assimilate and to renew the material which they have borrowed. We notice here the skill which Betjeman has employed to surpass the original. The tune is far more elaborate and delicate, the poem moves with an enchanting lyrical grace, the sensuous quality of the bells ringing out among the blossom is conveyed with perfect sureness of touch. The hymn is a decent piece of devotional verse, whereas Betjeman's canticle of praise attains the condition of poetry.

Before examining his poems in detail we should briefly consider the question of Betjeman's development. Some major artists appear to grow ever more complex and enigmatic, and it is possible to divide their work into clearly-defined periods which mark certain dramatic changes in their growth. Shakespeare, Beethoven, Van Gogh and Yeats are obvious examples of such artists. In the course of the twentieth century this empirical observation about the careers of some major artists has hardened into the dogma that all genuine artists develop in this way, and that they stand convicted of artistic immaturity, almost of moral turpitude, if they fail to remake their style and themselves as frequently as possible. Modernistic critical theory and the desire of the public-relations men to keep the market active have combined to inflate this theory of artistic development into an unquestioned axiom. Yet it does not work even for all major artists: in the field of English poetry, Pope, Wordsworth, Coleridge and Tennyson do not conform to the prescribed pattern. As for poets of slightly lesser stature, though still of the finest quality, the names of George Herbert, Marvell, Gray and Christina Rossetti may serve to show how constricting and presumptuous it is for critics to subject the natural growth of artists to some arbitrary theory of development.

Betjeman is an example of a writer whose career shows no spectacular development, no sudden leap into a new dimension. His poetry has indeed grown steadily more assured, subtle and moving as his experience of life and the range of his emotions have widened and deepened. The man and the artist have gained in wisdom and maturity, but the subject matter and formal pattern of the poetry have undergone no dramatic transformation. Betjeman continues to take delight in the themes which have always aroused his interest, and his poems still fall into a few categories which can be readily defined: satirical and light verse; narrative and anecdotal poems, often set in the nineteenth century and based on a historical event; personal poems about childhood, love and death; topographical poems, especially those in which he portrays landscapes, townscapes or seascapes with figures. Nor has he felt the impulse to discover a new poetic language or to make formal innovations, but has been content to inherit the idiom of his predecessors, inventing a few more tunes and composing variations on familiar themes. It will be convenient to look at Betjeman's poetry chronologically, to observe the changes in mood and emphasis from volume to volume, to notice how his mastery of tone, texture, metre and rhythm has increased over the years. We can, should the need arise, follow the thread of certain strands in his work from one volume to another and thus trace the emergence in his poetry of recurrent motifs. We may then be in a position to judge the significance of his poetry and to determine the nature of his achievement.

V. THE SHORTER POEMS

Mount Zion (1931) was published by a friend of Betjeman's who owned a small firm. Its typography, illustrations and pink and green paper mark it clearly as a book designed to be savoured by a small circle of initiates. The poems were prefaced by an illustration of Sezincote, a beautiful house in Gloucestershire where fashionable undergraduates of Oxford in the 1920s were regularly entertained. The volume bears a dedication typical of the spirit in which the whole enterprise is conceived:

> MRS ARTHUR DUGDALE
> therefore, the hostess of Sezincote, I run risk
> of alienating
> by dedicating to her this precious
> hyper-sophisticated book.

We can trace in this first volume many of the preoccupations and attitudes that recur throughout Betjeman's career: the element of parody ('Hymn'); the satirical portrait of business men ('The City'); the delight in making affectionate fun of a small town or a suburb portrayed with loving detail ('Camberley' and 'Westgate-on-Sea'); the recollection of a vanished way of life, obliterated by death ('Croydon'); the slightly macabre description of a death-bed ('Death in Leamington'). This latter poem characteristically relates the decay of a building to the physical dissolution of an old lady:

> Do you know that the stucco is peeling?
> Do you know that the heart will stop?
> From those yellow Italianate arches
> Do you hear the plaster drop?

Despite the obvious weaknesses of this first volume the exuberance and sense of fun still retain the power to amuse the reader. 'The 'Varsity Students' Rag' satirizes the snobbish mindlessness that animated undergraduates of the period who were both wealthy and rowdy. One does not need a detailed knowledge of the area around Piccadilly in the late twenties to appreciate the following stanza:

We had a rag at Monico's. *We* had a rag at the Troc.,
And the one we had at the Berkeley gave the customers
                                                    quite a shock.
Then we went to the Popular, and after that—oh my!
I *wish* you'd seen the rag we had in the Grill Room at the Cri.

Equally high-spirited, and more accomplished, is 'Competition', one of the nine poems from *Mount Zion* omitted from the *Collected Poems*. It recounts the eagerness of The Independent Calvinistic Methodist Chapel (1810), the Wesley Memorial Church (1860) and the Mount Carmel Baptists (Strict) (1875) to surpass one another in the splendour and modernity of their ecclesiastical furnishings:

The Gothic is bursting over the way
        With Evangelical Song,
For the pinnacled Wesley Memorial Church
        Is over a hundred strong,
And what is a New Jerusalem
        Gas-lit and yellow-wall'd
To a semi-circular pitchpine sea
        With electric-light install'd?

Continual Dew (1937), although aimed at a slightly wider audience than *Mount Zion*, may still be regarded as precious and hyper-sophisticated in its typography and general appearance, with a surrealistic dust-cover by McKnight Kauffer and imitation gilt clasps such as one used to find on prayer-books. It contains some of the poems from *Mount Zion* and a number of new poems. The subtitle, *A Little Book of Bourgeois Verse*, is a piece of self-mockery, but what of the main title? It is drawn from the Prayer for the Clergy and People, which is said in the Anglican order for Morning Prayer and for Evening Prayer:

Almighty and everlasting God, who alone workest great marvels; Send down upon our Bishops, and Curates, and all Congregations committed to their charge, the healthful Spirit of thy grace; and that they may truly please thee, pour upon them the continual dew of thy blessing.

It is difficult to fathom Betjeman's religious beliefs at this stage of his career, because his poems so often take refuge in an evasive irony. The subtitle of his first volume is *In Touch with the Infinite* and we are puzzled to know how seriously we should take it. And how are we meant to respond to a poem called 'Suicide on Junction Road Station after Abstention from Evening Communion in North London'? The jauntiness of the rhythm is at odds with the subject of the poem, and the final rhetorical question invites a ribald answer:

> Six on the upside! six on the down side!
> One gaslight in the Booking Hall
> And a thousand sins on this lonely station—
> What shall I do with them all?

In general, the volume marks an advance on *Mount Zion*, both in technical assurance and emotional maturity. Many of the poems are, indeed, little more than highly entertaining pieces of skilful *pastiche*. Even the deservedly famous 'The Arrest of Oscar Wilde at the Cadogan Hotel' is a thoroughly self-indulgent performance, perhaps appropriately so in that its protagonist exhibited similar traits. The arrest of Wilde by two plain-clothes policemen is presented as a mixture of melodrama and farce, and Betjeman cleverly avoids committing himself by adopting an ambiguous tone, deliberately playing up the absurd elements in the scene in order to conceal his own response to the tragedy of Wilde's downfall.

> 'Mr Woilde, we 'ave come for tew take yew
> Where felons and criminals dwell:
> We must ask yew tew leave with us quoietly
> For this *is* the Cadogan Hotel.'
>
> He rose, and he put down *The Yellow Book*.
> He staggered—and, terrible-eyed,
> He brushed past the palms on the staircase
> And was helped to a hansom outside.

One of the poems in the collection, 'Slough', has enjoyed a certain notoriety ever since it appeared:

> Come, friendly bombs, and fall on Slough
> It isn't fit for humans now,
> There isn't grass to graze a cow
> Swarm over, Death!

Betjeman's satirical and comic verses, which are dotted here and there throughout the *Collected Poems*, are the poems by which he is best known to the large majority of his readers. His satire is aimed at a wide variety of targets: profiteers, vulgar businessmen, progressives, hypocrites of every persuasion, bureaucrats, planners, brewers who modernize unpretentious inns. We have seen that some of his satirical prose is highly effective, and it is therefore disappointing that his verse satire is so comparatively feeble. Many facets of contemporary life arouse his keen dislike, and at times his irritation becomes intense; but he lacks the qualifications of a major satirical poet. The great masters of satire, such as Juvenal and Swift, exude an overpowering loathing of humanity, portraying men as monsters of cruelty and greed, depicting women as maenads given over to the pursuit of vicious luxury. Betjeman is incapable of viewing his fellow creatures as odious vermin, however nasty and stupid they sometimes appear to be. His natural kindness reinforces his Christian belief in the capacity of men to be redeemed, just as his awareness of mortality reminds him that we are all deserving of compassion because we are moving towards death. He cannot therefore follow the example of Yeats and study hatred with great diligence. It is impossible to believe that Betjeman genuinely wished Slough to be destroyed: one feels that he would have found it went against the grain to exult in the destruction of Sodom and Gomorrah.

Even the neatest of his satirical poems are deficient in the touch of savagery, the clinching power, that lend such virulent force to Chesterton's 'Antichrist' or Kipling's 'Gehazi'. The figures whom he attacks in 'Group Life: Letchworth', 'The Planster's Vision', 'The Town Clerk's Views', 'Huxley Hall' and 'The Dear Old Village' are men of straw. Two of his early satires, 'Bristol and Clifton' and 'In Westminster Abbey', were taken by some to be anti-Christian poems, although they are orthodox Christian attacks on certain aspects of Anglican formalism and obtuseness. Their impact, however, is so feeble that their purport is largely irrelevant.

The galumphing comic poems, which have been described as *New Statesman* competition poems, lack the redeeming features of the satires, and are scarcely worthy of mention. They afford a harmless pleasure, but they are small beer. Betjeman himself is more aware of the weaknesses inherent in his comic and satirical poems than are the anthologists who continue to reprint them. Referring specifically to 'Slough', 'In Westminster Abbey' and 'How to Get On in Society', he has remarked that 'they now seem to me merely comic verse and competent magazine writing, topical and tiresome'.

Many of his good poems, of course, are enchantingly funny and exhibit delightful flashes of satire, but the wit and the satire are subordinated to the main design and mood of the poem. Betjeman is at his most characteristic and moving when he is dwelling with loving particularity on a landscape or on a quirk of human nature, when he is remembering his childhood, or contemplating the way in which past and present mingle. Irritation and frustration may spur him into satirical verse, but he is stirred to write genuine poetry only when affection and compassion arouse the lyrical impulse.

This is true of 'Love in a Valley' and 'Death of King George V', the two poems in *Continual Dew* which unmistakably suggest that the period of Betjeman's juvenilia is drawing to its close. 'Love in a Valley' takes us for the first time into Betjeman country—the physical landscape of the Home Counties where the prosperous upper-middle classes have built their comfortable retreat:

> Deep down the drive go the cushioned rhododendrons,
> Deep down, sand deep, drives the heather root,
> Deep the spliced timber barked around the summer-house,
> Light lies the tennis-court, plantain underfoot.

We are also being introduced to Betjeman country in a metaphorical sense, to the world of amatory relations where Pam and Miss J. Hunter Dunn await us. In this earlier poem it is the girl who speaks:

> Take me, Lieutenant, to that Surrey homestead!
> Red comes the winter and your rakish car.

And the poem ends, unexpectedly, on a muted note:

> Leaded are the windows lozenging the crimson,
> Drained dark the pines in resin-scented rain.

Portable Lieutenant! they carry you to China
    And me to lonely shopping in a brilliant arcade;
Firm hand, fond hand, switch the giddy engine!
    So for us a last time is bright light made.

In 'Death of King George V', based on the *Daily Express*
headline, 'New King arrives in his capital by air', the
perception that Edward VIII's accession marked the passing
of an epoch is crystallized in a complex, vivid image:

Old men who never cheated, never doubted,
    Communicated monthly, sit and stare
At the new suburb stretched beyond the run-way
    Where a young man lands hatless from the air.

Further evidence of Betjeman's increasing mastery of his
medium is to be discerned in 'The Heart of Thomas Hardy',
a poem composed at this period and included in *Collected
Poems*, though not previously published in book form. The
tone is ambivalent, the concept behind it is odd to the point
of eccentricity; but the handling of the tricky metre is
exceptionally skilful, and one image is memorably grotesque:

Weighted down with a Conscience, now for the first time
                              fleshly
Taking form as a growth hung from the feet like a sponge-bag.
There, in the heart of the nimbus, twittered the heart of Hardy.

Old Lights for New Chancels (1940) reinforces the impres-
sion made by the more successful poems in *Continual Dew*.
The title 'A Shropshire Lad' suggests that we are in the
pastoral world of A. E. Housman, but the lad is Captain
Webb, who was born at Dawley in an industrial district of
that county, and the poem which, the author tells us, '*should
be recited with a Midland accent*', is a mock-serious ghost
story which moves to one of Betjeman's most captivating
tunes:

The gas was on in the Institute,
    The flare was up in the gym,
A man was running a mineral line,
    A lass was singing a hymn,
When Captain Webb the Dawley man,
    Captain Webb from Dawley,
Came swimming along in the old canal
    That carried the bricks to Lawley.

> Swimming along—
> Swimming along—
> Swimming along from Severn,
> And paying a call at Dawley bank while swimming along
> to Heaven.

Three or four poems strike a more sombre, wistful note than anything in the first two volumes. 'Oxford: Sudden Illness at the Bus-stop' is the first of many poems about North Oxford, dons and their wives, sickness and the intimations of mortality; 'Holy Trinity, Sloane Street' conjures up the atmosphere of early-twentieth-century Anglican Ritualism in Chelsea; 'On a Portrait of a Deaf Man', an elegy for Betjeman's father, plunges into that macabre preoccupation with the physical horror of death which Betjeman's faith seems powerless to exorcize.

The collection bears the subtitle *Verses Topographical and Amatory* (there is also a section labelled 'Miscellaneous'). Betjeman's amatory poems, although not among his finest achievements, have attracted much interest and praise. They certainly possess a unique flavour. One of the most celebrated appears in his 1940 volume, and its title 'Pot Pourri from a Surrey Garden' not only indicates the geographical setting but contains an oblique joke, since it is also the title of a late-Victorian book by Mrs C. W. Earle, a diary, with sections on gardening and cooking, dedicated to her sister, Lady Constance Lytton. Betjeman, in this poem, as in later poems, portrays himself as a Gulliver among the female Brobdingnagians: the emphasis is on the commanding strength of the girl, whose physical prowess and dominating character constitute a major part of her erotic fascination:

> See the strength of her arm, as firm and hairy as Hendren's;
>   See the size of her thighs, the pout of her lips as, cross,
> And full of a pent-up strength, she swipes at the
>   rhododendrons.

The reference to Hendren, a famous cricketer of the inter-war years, the deliberately outrageous rhyming, the dwelling on the formidable charms of the 'great big mountainous sports girl' all pile on the slightly perverse romantic agony, which culminates in marriage celebrated in a Victorian

Gothic Church, whose decoration is as cunningly elaborate as the poet's metrical pattern and extravagant rhymes:

> Over the redolent pinewoods, in at the bathroom casement,
> One fine Saturday, Windlesham bells shall call:
> Up the Butterfield aisle rich with Gothic enlacement,
> Licensed now for embracement,
> Pam and I, as the organ
> Thunders over you all.

It is amusing but perhaps irrelevant to wonder whether Betjeman is deliberately or unconsciously drawing on memories of *Dorothy: A Country Story* (1880) by A. J. Munby, who secretly married a servant-girl, and whose journal was published in 1972. The heroine of this poem springs from a much lower class than Pam, but physically and psychologically they are sisters under the rippling muscles:

> Oh, what a notable lass is our Dolly, the pride of the dairy!
> Stalwart and tall as a man, strong as a heifer to work:
> Built for beauty, indeed, but certainly built for labour—
> Witness her muscular arm, witness the grip of her hand.

Such Amazonian figures reappear in several poems in this and in subsequent volumes. We have Myfanwy, who is 'Strong and willowy, strong to pillow me', and who is apostrophized as

> my silken Myfanwy,
> Ringleader, tom-boy, and chum to the weak.

'A Subaltern's Love-song' celebrates the charms of Miss J. Hunter Dunn, who vanquishes the subaltern at tennis, and becomes engaged to him after they have sat in the car-park at Camberley during the Golf Club dance. Betjeman has told us that this poem records his feelings for a superintendent in the Ministry of Information canteen during the war, and although Betjeman has never been a subaltern he may have felt like one in his youth when he was seeking the hand of a Field-Marshal's daughter. 'The Olympic Girl' portrays yet another formidable young woman, a 'Fair tigress of the tennis courts'. The most accomplished poem in this category is 'The Licorice Fields at Pontefract', which

33

begins as an irreverent parody of Yeats's 'Down by the Sally-Garden':

> In the licorice fields at Pontefract
> My love and I did meet

Yet, in the final stanza, which once again casts the poet in the role of the weak male dominated by the powerful woman, the sophisticated self-mockery is consumed in a sudden flare of eroticism. This embracement is certainly unlicensed:

> She cast her blazing eyes on me
> And plucked a licorice leaf;
> I was her captive slave and she
> My red-haired robber chief.
> Oh love! for love I could not speak,
> It left me winded, wilting, weak
> And held in brown arms strong and bare
> And wound with flaming ropes of hair.

Elsewhere, notably in 'Senex' and still more in 'Late-Flowering Lust', sexual desire is linked with the horror of physical decay, with a vision of two skeletons:

> Dark sockets look on emptiness
> Which once was loving-eyed,
> The mouth that opens for a kiss
> Has got no tongue inside.

One poem in *Old Lights for New Chancels*, 'Trebetherick', hints at reserves of lyrical delicacy and power which may have astonished some admirers of Betjeman:

> But when a storm was at its height,
> And feathery slate was black in rain,
> And tamarisks were hung with light
> And golden sand was brown again,
> Spring tide and blizzard would unite
> And sea came flooding up the lane.

This lyrical vein runs through *New Bats in Old Belfries* (1945) and reappears in some of the half-dozen poems published for the first time in *Selected Poems* (1948). The opening lines of 'Before the Anaesthetic, *or* A Real Fright' reveal Betjeman's accomplishment as a landscape artist:

Intolerably sad, profound
St Giles's bells are ringing round,
They bring the slanting summer rain
To tap the chestnut boughs again
Whose shadowy cave of rainy leaves
The gusty belfry-song receives.

The sea, particularly the Cornish coast, and memories of childhood are among the most potent sources of poetry for Betjeman. Two poems in blank verse, 'Sunday Afternoon Service in St Enodoc Church, Cornwall' and 'North Coast Recollections', spring from the confluence of these two sources, and exemplify the poet's mastery of an exacting medium. The echoes of eighteenth- and nineteenth-century writers may appear to detract from Betjeman's originality, but at the same time they form an essential part of the pleasure which the poems yield. One of the finest passages of 'Sunday Afternoon Service' is the long paragraph which concludes the poem, too long to quote in full. A brief extract may suggest something of its quality but cannot do justice to the poet's command of syntax, tone and change of pace, which have traditionally been the hallmark of poetic intelligence:

Where deep cliffs loom enormous, where cascade
Mesembryanthemum and stone-crop down,
Where the gull looks no larger than a lark
Hung midway twixt the cliff-top and the sand,
Sun-shadowed valleys roll along the sea.
Forced by the backwash, see the nearest wave
Rise to a wall of huge, translucent green
And crumble into spray along the top
Blown seaward by the land-breeze.

The closing lines of 'North Coast Recollections' attain an equally firm amplitude, although they are less concerned with the minute particulars of the seascape than with its emotional resonance:

Then pealing out across the estuary
The Padstow bells rang up for practice-night
An undersong to birds and dripping shrubs.
The full Atlantic at September spring
Flooded a final tide-mark up the sand,

> And ocean sank to silence under bells,
> And the next breaker was a lesser one
> Then lesser still. Atlantic, bells and birds
> Were layer on interchanging layer of sound.

Yet, despite Betjeman's deft craftmanship as a writer of blank verse, he is at his best and most characteristic when his lyrical impulse is quickened by the challenge of rhyme-schemes and stanzaic patterns. The more intricate the tune the more nimbly and inventively his imagination dances, the more daringly he fuses a variety of emotions into a poetic unity. In 'Henley-on-Thames' the pastoral idyll is saved from sinking into an inertly sentimental reverie by the solidity of the two stalwart young women, members of the Auxiliary Territorial Service, and also by the lithe movement of the verse:

> When shall I see the Thames again?
> The prow-promoted gems again,
>> As beefy ATS
>> Without their hats
> Come shooting through the bridge?
>> And 'cheerioh' and 'cheeri-bye'
>> Across the waste of waters die,
>> And low the mists of evening lie
> And lightly skims the midge.

Betjeman was well advised to abandon the use of blank verse until he required it for the special purposes of his autobiography. His metrical skill attains a full maturity in *New Bats in Old Belfries* in a dozen haunting poems.

The publication of *A Few Late Chrysanthemums* (1954) dispelled any lingering suspicions that Betjeman was not a serious artist. The good poems come so thick and fast that any appraisal of the volume runs the risk of degenerating into a laudatory catalogue. It may be more helpful to devote some detailed attention to one poem, and to refer to a couple of other poems, rather than attempt a summary of the whole collection.

'Middlesex' brings together many of the strands which we have traced in the prose and in the earlier poems: Betjeman's ability to be funny, tender and lyrical simultaneously; his delight in recording minutiae of class dis-

tinctions and social habits; his nostalgia for the vanished
world of his childhood and of vintage London; his complex
response to the collocation of past and present; his sense of
mortality and of the pathos of human life vividly recalled to
our eyes and hearts by the image of the great London
cemeteries.

The poem opens with two stanzas devoted to a description
of Elaine's return, presumably from work in Central
London, to her suburban home. Just as Eliot in *The Waste
Land* contrasts the love stories of the legendary Iseult and
Queen Elizabeth I with the seduction of the typist, so
Betjeman ironically depicts a modern girl whose name is
Tennysonian but whose way of life is lower-middle class:

> Gaily into Ruislip Gardens
>   Runs the red electric train,
> With a thousand Ta's and Pardon's
>   Daintily alights Elaine;
> Hurries down the concrete station
> With a frown of concentration,
> Out into the outskirt's edges
> Where a few surviving hedges
> Keep alive our lost Elysium—rural Middlesex again.
>
> Well cut Windsmoor flapping lightly,
>   Jacqmar scarf of mauve and green
> Hiding hair which, Friday nightly,
>   Delicately drowns in Drene;
> Fair Elaine the bobby-soxer,
> Fresh-complexioned with Innoxa,
> Gains the garden—father's hobby—
> Hangs her Windsmoor in the lobby,
> Settles down to sandwich supper and the television screen.

The irony is affectionate; the description of her home life is
gently satirical; the names of the branded clothes, shampoo
and cosmetic are recounted with a humorous relish almost
as if they constitute a Homeric roll-call. Then the poem
changes mood and direction, as the third stanza pivots away
from the built-up suburb of the 1950s to the lost Elysium
of Betjeman's childhood:

> Gentle Brent, I used to know you
>   Wandering Wembley-wards at will,

Now what change your waters show you
        In the meadowlands you fill!
Recollect the elm-trees misty
And the footpaths climbing twisty
Under cedar-shaded palings,
Low laburnum-leaned-on railings,
Out of Northolt on and upward to the heights of Harrow hill.

In the final stanza Betjeman fills his landscape with figures
from *The Diary of a Nobody* (1892), a late-Victorian work
of fiction by George and Weedon Grossmith. The last four
lines transport us to a remote world where archaic licensing
laws provide for the needs of *bona fide* travellers, and where
the 'cockney anglers, cockney shooters' stand out in their
sharp, quirky individuality against the blurred masses of
our consumer society. The long amplitude of the con-
cluding line evokes what Betjeman has called 'that most
Victorian sight of all London—the windy Carrara-covered
cemetery'. Elaine, unlike Murray Posh and Lupin Pooter,
will end up in the crematorium, delivered there in a Co-
operative funeral van:

Parish of enormous hayfields
        Perivale stood all alone,
And from Greenford scent of mayfields
        Most enticingly was blown
Over market gardens tidy,
Taverns for the *bona fide*,
Cockney anglers, cockney shooters,
Murray Poshes, Lupin Pooters
Long in Kensal Green and Highgate silent under soot and stone.

We may resent Betjeman's air of kindly condescension
towards Elaine, and argue that she is in no way inferior to
the characters affectionately portrayed by the Grossmiths.
The poem can be read as an example of Betjeman's nostalgia
for the days when sweated labour, cheap domestic help and
the laws of a rigidly hierarchical society kept his parents in
comfort and the workers in their proper station. 'The
Metropolitan Railway', another poem which juxtaposes
past and present, lacks the element of mild snobbery and
patrician irony which tinges 'Middlesex'. The irony in
'The Metropolitan Railway' is tender, and is directed against

a married couple of his own class whose youthful dreams have faded since Edwardian days. Again we find ourselves in 'autumn-scented Middlesex', but only for a moment: the emotional heart of the poem is Baker Street Station, with its 'many-branched electrolier' under which perhaps 'your parents' met one evening at six-fifteen and caught the train to that lost Elysium. When the poem returns to the present day we learn of the desolation that the years have made, and see the dark side of fair Elaine's world for the survivors of Edwardian England:

> Cancer has killed him. Heart is killing her.
>   The trees are down. An Odeon flashes fire
> Where stood their villa by the murmuring fir.

A third poem which counterpoises the vanished and vanquished world of the past against the vulgar present is 'The Old Liberals'. The opening lines conjure up an interior which is gracious yet a shade pedantic and eccentric, the ghostly relic of an epoch when Robert Bridges compiled his hymns at Yattendon and the dreams of William Morris still lingered on among the dwindling groups of his disciples:

> Pale green of the *English Hymnal*! Yattendon hymns
>   Played on the *hautbois* by a lady dress'd in blue
>   Her white-hair'd father accompanying her thereto
> On tenor or bass-recorder.

Betjeman knows that such people are defeated, and in lamenting their fate he is mourning a part of his youth, a lost dream of England, banished by a harsher, uglier world:

> Where are the wains with garlanded swathes a-swaying?
> Where are the swains to wend through the lanes-a-maying?
>   Where are the blithe and jocund to ted the hay?
>   Where are the free folk of England? Where are they?
>
> Ask of the Abingdon bus with full load creeping
>   Down into denser suburbs.

Betjeman divided *A Few Late Chrysanthemums* into three sections, 'Medium', 'Gloom' and 'Light'. His article in *The Spectator*, 8 October 1954, which contains an answer to certain of his readers who regretted the presence of so much encircling gloom, provides a valuable gloss on his temperamental endowment and on his emotional development since his days at Oxford:

In those days my purest pleasure was the exploration of suburbs and provincial towns and my impurest pleasure the pursuit of the brawny athletic girl. When most of the poems in my latest book were written, I was the self-pitying victim of remorse, guilt and terror of death. Much as I dislike trying to conform to Christian morality . . . the only practical way to face the dreaded lonely journey into Eternity seems to me the Christian one. I therefore try to believe that Christ was God, made man and gives Eternal Life, and that I may be confirmed in this belief by clinging to the sacraments and by prayer . . . For there is no doubt that fear of death (a manifestation of the lack of faith I deeply desire), remorse and a sense of man's short time on earth and an impatience with so-called 'progress', did inform many of the poems in my latest volume. Since then I have grown a little more cheerful and thankful and hope to produce some poems expressing the joys of being alive.

Betjeman has for many years combined a genuine Anglican piety with a gnawing uncertainty about the truth of Christianity, and it is arguable that this fruitful ambivalence gives many of his poems a keen poignancy and a finely-poised delicacy which a more robust assurance would blunt and coarsen. His beloved Thomas Hardy disbelieved in the Christmas story yet hoped that it might be true; Betjeman affirms his faith in it while fearing that it may be false. Even in 'Christmas', one of his most serene and unaffected expressions of Christian devotion, the last three stanzas, which proclaim the wonders of the Incarnation, ask three times the question 'And is it true?' and answer in the conditional tense 'For if it is . . . '

Betjeman's output of lyrical poems since *A Few Late Chrysanthemums* has not been large. *Collected Poems* (1958), which brought him so remarkable and unexpected a measure of popular applause, contains most of the contents of *Mount Zion* and of *Continual Dew*, almost every poem from the subsequent volumes, one from *Poems in the Porch* (1954), a pamphlet in verse about church matters, and nineteen hitherto uncollected. The third edition (1970) incorporates eight poems from earlier books added to the 1962 edition and all from *High and Low* (1966), a work in four sections, 'Landscapes', 'Portraits', 'Light and Dark' and 'Personal'.

Many of the poems written between 1954 and 1966 record the poet's deepening awareness of change and decay, mortality and the passing of the old order. In 'Good-bye' and 'Five o'Clock Shadow' the physical horror of death is apprehended so fiercely that the artistic distancing and impersonality which an achieved poem requires are distorted and overwhelmed. Much more successful are the poems in which the recollection of beloved scenes and of past happiness counterpoises the lamentation and the fear. Yet in such poems the dominant note is still one of sadness, of regret that the modern world is more brutal and ugly than the one which it has superseded. In 'Monody on the Death of Aldersgate Street Station' the remembrance of church bells in the City cannot avert the desecration of London, and the closing of Aldersgate Street Station symbolizes both the destruction of Vintage London and the declining powers of the poet and his coevals:

> Snow falls in the buffet of Aldersgate station,
> Toiling and doomed from Moorgate Street puffs the train,
> For us of the steam and the gas-light, the lost generation,
> The new white cliffs of the City are built in vain.

Even the ostensibly lighter poems may take a sinister turn. 'Winthrop Mackworth Redivivus', written in the metre of Praed's most scintillating poem, 'Goodnight to the Season', starts off in a vein of highly entertaining satire, which dissects with deadly accuracy the foibles of a silly, snobbish woman:

> And plants for indoors are the fashion—
>   Or so the *News Chronicle* said—
> So I've ventured some housekeeping cash on
>   A cactus which seems to be dead.
> An artist with whom we're acquainted
>   Has stippled the dining-room stove
> And the walls are alternately painted
>   Off-yellow and festival mauve.

Yet we learn in the fourth stanza that the woman's daughter, Matilda, appears to harbour the delusion that she is a horse.

The jokey tone of the poem merely intensifies the desolation of a household where the parents, who pride themselves on being cultured and highly rational, resort in vain to psycho-analysis and to a Riding School, in the hope of healing their daughter's spiritual unease, and wonder, in despair, whether the Church might be called in to exorcize something—the poverty-stricken vagueness of the word evokes the hollow uncertainty of the speaker.

In some of the Cornish poems with which *High and Low* opens, an affirmative faith dissipates for a moment the melancholy reflections. 'Winter Seascape' ends with the poet's surveying 'a huge consoling sea'; in 'Old Friends' his sadness at the thought of vanished friends is lightened by a sense that we may enjoy communion with the dead:

> As I reach our hill, I am part of a sea unseen—
> The oppression lifts.

But 'Tregardock', perhaps the finest poem in the collection, moves from a quietly menacing exordium towards a climax in which the poet anatomizes with exultant savagery the cowardice that makes him resist the lure of self-destruction:

> The dunlin do not move, each bird
> Is stationary on the sand
> As if a spirit in it heard
> The final end of Sea and land.

> And I on my volcano edge
> Exposed to ridicule and hate
> Still do not dare to leap the ledge
> And smash to pieces on the slate.

Two of Betjeman's most powerful later poems[1] revert to his preoccupation with death and eternity. 'N.W.5 & N.6' evokes memories of his childhood and of the way in which a nursery-maid's talk of damnation, 'world without end', communicated to the child, as the church bells rang out through the late evening sky,

> her fear
> And guilt at endlessness. I caught them too,
> Hating to think of sphere succeeding sphere
> Into eternity and God's dread will.
> I caught her terror then. I have it still.

[1] From *Collected Poems*.

'Felixstowe, or The Last of Her Order', one of many poems in which Betjeman conveys his sympathy for the old and the lonely, is a monologue by the last survivor of 'The Little Sisters of the Hanging Pyx', an order founded in 1894. As so often in Betjeman the changing moods of the sea awaken a flood of emotion, and the minute external particulars of Felixstowe—'the cushioned scabious', 'a cakeshop's tempting scones', 'the red brick twilight of St John's'—are dwelt on lingeringly in the hope that a turbulent uncertainty and fear may be allayed. The final avowal of faith, with its emphasis on safety, its repeated claim that inner peace has been attained, suggests the desperate need of the speaker for comfort and reassurance:

> Safe from the vain world's silly sympathising,
>   Safe with the Love that I was born to know,
> Safe from the surging of the lonely sea
> My heart finds rest, my heart finds rest in Thee.

The whole body of Betjeman's poetry charts the oscillation between the terror experienced by the child in North London and the faith that clings to belief in God as death draws near.

Although he has published no collection since *High and Low*, Betjeman has continued to write poems on his favourite themes. 'The Newest Bath Guide', an imitation of Christopher Anstey's satirical poem *The New Bath Guide* (1766), reflects his love of pastiche and his detestation of the speculators and the bureaucrats who are destroying yet another beautiful city:

> Goodbye to old Bath. We who loved you are sorry
> They've carted you off by developer's lorry.

He has indulged in his fondness for Victoriana and for pastiche by composing sonnets feigned to have been written by the lovesick heroine of *The Barrier* (1973), Robin Maugham's novel about late-nineteenth-century India. *The Sunday Express* published on 13 May 1973 a new poem by Betjeman, 'Lenten Thoughts of a High Anglican', about an unknown woman whom he glimpsed in church and whom he calls 'The Mistress'. It contains one characteristic simile:

> And the sound of her voice is deep and low
> Like the Christ Church tenor bell.

Yet she in no way resembles Pam or Miss J. Hunter Dunn; neither does her sexual attractiveness drag in its train the associations of lust and death which sometimes attend Betjeman's poems about carnal love. For once, Betjeman is nearer to D. H. Lawrence's mysticism about sex than to the mistrust of the flesh traditionally fostered by the Pauline strain in Christian morality:

> I hope that the preacher will not think
> It unorthodox and odd
> If I add that I glimpse in The Mistress
> A hint of The Unknown God.

VI. *SUMMONED BY BELLS*

Betjeman's long autobiographical poem, *Summoned by Bells* (1960), stands apart from the rest of his work. This account of his life from early childhood down to his departure from Oxford is written in a medium which he had hitherto essayed in only three poems. His prefatory note explains the reason for his choice of blank verse:

The author has gone as near prose as he dare. He chose blank verse, for all but the more hilarious moments, because he found it best suited to brevity and the rapid changes of mood and subject.

Evelyn Waugh's acerb comment in his diary on *Summoned by Bells* is characteristically bitter and unfair:

John demonstrates how much more difficult it is to write blank verse than jingles and raises the question: *why* did he not go into his father's workshop? It would be far more honourable and useful to make expensive ashtrays than to appear on television and just as lucrative.

Yet Waugh displays his habitual acuteness in perceiving that the subtle constraints of blank verse are less welcome to Betjeman's poetic sensibility than the challenges of rhyme and metrical patterns. It is a readable, enjoyable poem, which affords us an interesting account of the poet's childhood and adolescence, of his growing estrangement from his father, of his first gropings towards religious faith, of his 'sense of guilt increasing with the years'. The most memorable passages are those describing the hideous bullyings organized with ritual cruelty at Marlborough, and those which recount his lifelong perplexity about the central doctrine of Christianity:

> What seemed to me a greater question then
> Tugged and still tugs. Is Christ the Son of God? . . .
> Some know for all their lives that Christ is God,
> Some start upon that arduous love affair
> In clouds of doubt and argument; and some
> (My closest friends) seem not to want His love—
> And why this is I wish to God I knew.

Summoned by Bells suffers from the fact that it appears to be covering familiar ground, because the autobiographical element in the collected poems is so strong and vivid. Yet the verse autobiography contains a great deal of fresh material and goes into detail about a number of matters which are merely glanced at in the remainder of Betjeman's work. It is a measure of the book's merits and limitations that, although admirers of Betjeman will value it for its intrinsic quality as well as for the light which it sheds on the man and the poet, *Summoned by Bells* is not a volume that one would recommend to anybody unacquainted with the author's shorter poems.

VII. CONCLUSION

Betjeman's achievement remains a matter for discussion, which can speedily degenerate into acrimonious debate. Some of his severe critics hold him up to scorn as a cult figure promoted to an undeservedly high status by smart journalists; and cite his career as an example of the way in which the upper-middle-class network of metropolitan London promulgates a false set of cultural values. On this view Betjeman is nothing more than a twentieth-century Praed or Tom Moore, a licensed jester of the Establishment who has contrived to flatter the prejudices of sophisticated readers

45

and, at the same time, to catch the eyes and ears of television viewers who wish to be thought sophisticated. This would in itself be a feat demanding at the very least a remarkable degree of sheer cleverness and virtuosity; but it would invalidate his claims to be regarded as a serious artist.

Those who are tempted to dismiss Betjeman in such a cavalier fashion may pause and recall that he has never lacked admirers among fine critics and poets of widely different generations and tastes. In 1958 Edmund Wilson remarked that, apart from Auden and Dylan Thomas, Betjeman was the most interesting English poet since T. S. Eliot. W. H. Auden's preface to *Slick but not Streamlined* celebrates the skill and originality of the poet to whom he dedicated *The Age of Anxiety*. More recently, Philip Larkin has written a brilliant introduction to the 1971 American edition of Betjeman's *Collected Poems*, in which he makes very large claims about Betjeman's place in the history of twentieth-century poetry, claims reinforced by the amount of space allotted to him in Larkin's anthology, *The Oxford Book of Twentieth-Century English Verse* (1973).

We need not accept Larkin's extremely high estimate of Betjeman. In particular we may view with scepticism his belief that Betjeman's poetic stature and significance are comparable with Eliot's. Larkin ingeniously supports his argument by quoting from Eliot's *Notes Towards the Definition of Culture* (1948) a passage which lists the properties of our 'whole way of life':

Derby Day, Henley Regatta, Cowes, the twelfth of August, a cup final, the pin table, the dartboard, Wensleydale cheese, boiled cabbage cut in sections, beetroot in vinegar, nineteenth-century Gothic churches, and the music of Elgar.

As Larkin observes, 'if this passage reminds us of anyone's poetry, it is Betjeman's rather than Eliot's or anyone else's'. Yet we do not habitually turn to the major poets if we want to inform ourselves about the properties, the accidents, of a civilization. Tennyson, Arnold and Hopkins reveal to us profound truths about the mind and heart of Victorian England, but we must go elsewhere, to minor writers and journalists, for detailed accounts of Victorian social habits, furnishings and fashions. W. B. Yeats, T. S. Eliot and D. H. Lawrence interpret to us the profound currents of thought and emotion during the first half of our century, yet they tell us little about the appurtenances of our civilization.

Betjeman does not, for all his variety, and his keenness of social observation, give us a powerful and comprehensive vision of society, or a sustained argument about the nature of man. While it is not true that he is indifferent or unsympathetic to the poor, he shows little understanding of the political and social aspirations which animate large numbers of the working classes. Even his religious preoccupations are individualistic: he broods intensely on his own death and the death of his friends; he longs for salvation after death for himself and those he loves, rather than for the redemption of all mankind, the renewal of the creation.

Yet these very limitations, this fidelity to his temperament and to his experience, this refusal to pretend, give his poems a rare grace and authenticity. He is, moreover, a lyrical poet of singular purity, whose mastery of the singing line and of melodic flow enables him to compose a variety of enchanting tunes. In 'Ireland with Emily', his finest tribute to the country which has fascinated him since his Oxford days, he describes with an exuberant wit the decaying beauty of a ruined abbey:

> There in pinnacled protection,
>   One extinguished family waits
> A Church of Ireland resurrection
>   By the broken, rusty gates.
> Sheepswool, straw and droppings cover
> Graves of spinster, rake and lover,
> Whose fantastic mausoleum
> Sings its own seablown Te Deum,
>   In and out the slipping slates.

He can suggest, with equal felicity, a very different ambience in which the lower-middle-class mother of five drags her way round the crowded stores and queues up for rationed goods :

> But her place is empty in the queue at the International,
>   The greengrocer's queue lacks one,

So does the crowd at MacFisheries. There is no one to go to
                                                    Freeman's
    To ask if the shoes are done.

The command of metre and rhythm in that poem, 'Variation
on a Theme by T. W. Rolleston', is surpassed in the superb
elegy for Walter Ramsden of Pembroke College, Oxford,
which moves to one of Betjeman's most cunning tunes. He
conveys within a tiny compass the sadness of the three old
Fellows of the College who survive Walter Ramsden and
who recall the distant summers and the long-dead rowing
men returning to celebrate their feats on the river. The
observation of detail, the evocation of mood, the control
of tone are masterly:

    They remember, as the coffin to its final obsequations
        Leaves the gates,
    Buzz of bees in window boxes on their summer ministrations,
        Kitchin din,
        Cups and plates,
    And the getting of bump suppers[1] for the long-dead
                                                    generations
        Coming in,
        From Eights.

Despite Betjeman's metrical adroitness he has not felt the
need to make the kind of radical innovation in poetic
technique which has distinguished the work of Pound, Eliot
and Lawrence. Those who reproach Betjeman for his innate
conservatism will find it salutary to reflect on the words put
by Chekhov into Treplev's mouth in *The Seagull*:

I have come more and more to believe that it is not a question
of new and old forms, but that what matters is that a man should
write without thinking about forms at all, write because it
springs freely from his soul.

As Leslie Stephen remarks in his essay, 'Gray and his School',
the ultimate aim of the poet should be to touch our hearts by

---

[1] To celebrate the achievement of a number of 'bumps' in Eights Week,
when the college eight-oared boats race in single file up the narrow river,
any boat touching the stern of the competitor ahead taking its place on
the following day.

showing his own, and not to exhibit his learning, or his fine taste, or his skill in mimicking the notes of his predecessors.

No contemporary poet has displayed more skill than Betjeman in composing variations on traditional themes, yet his best poetry fulfils the conditions laid down by Leslie Stephen.

One of Betjeman's finest though comparatively unfamiliar poems, 'The Cottage Hospital', is worth quoting in full to demonstrate his power to touch our hearts. It is a fair criticism of much of his work to say that its appeal is limited to those who share its cultural background (although most good poets yield more pleasure if we are prepared to attune ourselves to their range of knowledge and sensibility). 'The Cottage Hospital' makes no such demands upon its readers, even if it is mildly useful to know that a cottage hospital normally serves a rural district. We need to bring nothing to the poem, whose theme is universal, except an alert intelligence and a candid heart. Betjeman's poems usually employ a traditional narrative or logical order, unlike poetry of the modernist movement which relies on the logic of images, the auditory imagination, the quasi-musical progression. In this poem Betjeman adopts some of the devices of symbolism: there is no logical connexion between the fly trapped in the spider's web and Betjeman's death as envisaged in the final stanza; and we are left to discern for ourselves the links between the sets of images, to respond to the poem's emotional development. 'The Cottage Hospital' abounds in felicitous touches. The adjective 'fizzing', usually associated with the opening of champagne or ginger beer bottles, takes on a grim association when applied to the auditory and the visual aspects of the buzzing fly's hopeless struggle. 'Inflexible nurses' feet' brilliantly mimes not only the tap of heels on the parquet but also the attitude of the nurses, whose impersonal sympathy must seem like indifference to the dying man, an indifference no less cruel than that displayed by everything in the garden to the dying insect. Yet the drift towards self-pity is halted. Betjeman does not dwell exclusively on the horror of physical dissolution, but recognizes that during his death agony the cycle of natural growth

49

will continue, that, in every generation, children play on, unmindful of the suffering around them, and that in the midst of death we are in life:

At the end of a long-walled garden
    in a red provincial town,
A brick path led to a mulberry—
    scanty grass at its feet.
I lay under blackening branches
    where the mulberry leaves hung down
Sheltering ruby fruit globes
    from a Sunday-tea-time heat.
Apple and plum espaliers
    basked upon bricks of brown;
The air was swimming with insects,
    and children played in the street.

Out of this bright intentness
    into the mulberry shade
Musca domestica (housefly)
    swung from the August light
Slap into slithery rigging
    by the waiting spider made
Which spun the lithe elastic
    till the fly was shrouded tight.
Down came the hairy talons
    and horrible poison blade
And none of the garden noticed
    that fizzing, hopeless fight.

Say in what Cottage Hospital
    whose pale green walls resound
With the tap upon polished parquet
    of inflexible nurses' feet
Shall I myself be lying
    when they range the screens around?
And say shall I groan in dying,
    as I twist the sweaty sheet?
Or gasp for breath uncrying,
    as I feel my senses drown'd
While the air is swimming with insects
    and children play in the street ?

JOHN BETJEMAN

A Select Bibliography

(Place of publication London, unless stated otherwise)

Collections:

SLICK BUT NOT STREAMLINED; New York (1947)
—a selection of verse and prose, selected and with an introduction by
W. H. Auden.

SELECTED POEMS (1948)
—chosen and with a preface by John Sparrow.

COLLECTED POEMS (1958)
—compiled and with an introduction by the Earl of Birkenhead; 2nd
ed., 1962; 3rd enlarged ed., 1970.

SELECTED POEMS (1958)
—in the 'Pocket Poets' series. The editor's name is not indicated.

A RING OF BELLS (1962)
—poems introduced and selected by Irene Slade. A selection intended
for children.

COLLECTED POEMS; Boston, Mass. (1971)
—enlarged ed., with a preface by Philip Larkin.

Separate Works:

MOUNT ZION; or, In Touch with the Infinite [1931]. *Verse*
—this publication bears no date, but the copy in the Bodleian Library,
Oxford is marked as having been received on 19 December 1931.

GHASTLY GOOD TASTE (1933). *Architecture*
—revised and with a new introduction by the author, 1970.

CONTINUAL DEW: A Little Book of Bourgeois Verse (1937). *Verse*

SIR JOHN PIERS; Mullingar [1938]. *Verse Pamphlet*
—published under the pseudonym 'Epsilon'. This poem is reprinted
in *Old Lights for New Chancels*, 1940, and in *Collected Poems*, 1958.

AN OXFORD UNIVERSITY CHEST (1938). *Architecture and Social History*
—facsimile reprint, 1970.

ANTIQUARIAN PREJUDICE (1939). *Architecture*
—a Hogarth Pamphlet. Reprinted in *First and Last Loves*, 1952.

OLD LIGHTS FOR NEW CHANCELS: Verses Topographical and Amatory
(1940). *Verse*

VINTAGE LONDON (1942). *Topography*

ENGLISH CITIES AND SMALL TOWNS (1943). *Architecture*
—in the 'Britain in Pictures' series.

JOHN PIPER (1944). *Art Criticism*
—an illustrated monograph in the 'Penguin Modern Painters' series.

NEW BATS IN OLD BELFRIES (1945). *Verse*

FIRST AND LAST LOVES (1952). *Architecture*
—a selection of essays.

A FEW LATE CHRYSANTHEMUMS (1954). *Verse*

POEMS IN THE PORCH (1954). *Verse pamphlet*
—part of the author's note runs: 'These verses do not pretend to be
poetry. They were written for speaking on the wireless, and went
out over the Western Region.' Illustrations by John Piper. One
poem, 'Diary of a Church Mouse', is reprinted in *Collected Poems*.

THE ENGLISH TOWN IN THE LAST HUNDRED YEARS; Cambridge (1956).
Architecture
—the Rede Lecture, delivered at the Senate House, Cambridge,
9 May 1956.

SUMMONED BY BELLS (1960). *Verse autobiography*

GROUND PLAN TO SKYLINE (1960). *Architecture*
—published under the pseudonym 'Richard M. Farran'. The Bodleian
Library at Oxford possesses a letter from John Betjeman acknow-
ledging his authorship of this work.

HIGH AND LOW (1966). *Verse*

A PICTORIAL HISTORY OF ENGLISH ARCHITECTURE (1972). *Architecture*

LONDON'S HISTORIC RAILWAY STATIONS (1972). *Architecture*

WEST COUNTRY CHURCHES (1973). *Architecture*

Works Edited or Containing Contributions by John Betjeman:
CORNWALL ILLUSTRATED (1934). *Topography*
—enlarged ed., 1964. A Shell Guide.

DEVON [1936]. *Topography*
—a Shell Guide. Reissued and revised, 1939 and 1955.

ENGLISH, SCOTTISH AND WELSH LANDSCAPE, 1700-c.1860 (1944). *Verse
anthology*
—in collaboration with Geoffrey Taylor.

MURRAY'S BUCKINGHAMSHIRE ARCHITECTURAL GUIDE (1948). *Architecture*
—in collaboration with John Piper.

MURRAY'S BERKSHIRE ARCHITECTURAL GUIDE (1949). *Architecture*
—in collaboration with John Piper.

SHROPSHIRE (1951). *Topography*
—in collaboration with John Piper. A Shell Guide.

GALA DAY (1953). *Topographical Miscellany*
—Photographs by I. Bidermanas. Texts by a variety of hands. Contains two short uncollected poems by John Betjeman.

ENGLISH LOVE POEMS (1957). *Verse anthology*
—in collaboration with Geoffrey Taylor.
COLLINS GUIDE TO ENGLISH PARISH CHURCHES (1958). *Architecture*
—edited and with a long introduction by John Betjeman.
ALTAR AND PEW: Church of England Verses (1959). *Verse anthology*
—edited and with an introduction by John Betjeman. In the 'Pocket
Poets' series.
A HUNDRED SONNETS: [by] Charles Tennyson Turner (1960). *Verse
anthology*
—selected and with an introduction by John Betjeman and Sir Charles
Tennyson.
ENGLISH CHURCHES (1964). *Architecture*
—edited by Basil Clarke and John Betjeman. Text by Basil Clarke,
illustrations mainly chosen by John Betjeman.
VICTORIAN AND EDWARDIAN LONDON FROM OLD PHOTOGRAPHS (1969).
Topography
—introduction and commentary by John Betjeman.
VICTORIAN AND EDWARDIAN OXFORD FROM OLD PHOTOGRAPHS (1971).
Topography
—selected by John Betjeman and David Vaisey. Introduction by John
Betjeman.
VICTORIAN AND EDWARDIAN BRIGHTON FROM OLD PHOTOGRAPHS (1972).
Topography
—selected by John Betjeman and J. S. Gray. Introduction by John
Betjeman.
THE ART OF IVY COMPTON BURNETT, ed. C. Burkhart (1972). *Symposium*
—contains a short review of *A Father and His Fate* reprinted from
The Daily Telegraph, 16 August 1957.

Some Critical Studies:
JOHN BETJEMAN: A Study, by D. Stanford (1961)
—contains some valuable material and some interesting photographs.
RONALD FIRBANK and JOHN BETJEMAN, by J. Brooke (1962)
—in the 'Writers and their Work' series.
JOHN BETJEMAN AND DORSET, by L. Sieveking (1963)
—an account by the producer of John Betjeman's early broadcasting
of 'Dorset' and 'Westgate-on-Sea'.
INDEPENDENT ESSAYS, by J. Sparrow (1963)
—contains an essay on John Betjeman, which is an expansion of the
Preface to *Selected Poems* (1948), and which incorporates material
from the unsigned review in *The Times Literary Supplement*,
12 December 1958.
MEMORIES, 1898-1939, by C. M. Bowra (1966)
—recalls Betjeman at Oxford and in the early 1930s.

'It could only happen in England', by Philip Larkin, *The Cornhill Magazine*, No. 1069, Autumn 1971.

—written as a preface for the 1971 American edition of John Betjeman's enlarged *Collected Poems*. It contains some material from Larkin's review of *Collected Poems* (1958) in *Listen*, VIII, ii, Spring 1959.

WRITERS AND THEIR WORK

SWIFT: J. Middleton Murry
SIR JOHN VANBRUGH: Bernard Harris
HORACE WALPOLE: Hugh Honour

Nineteenth Century:

MATTHEW ARNOLD: Kenneth Allott
JANE AUSTEN: S. Townsend Warner
BAGEHOT: N. St John-Stevas
THE BRONTËS: I & II:
                Winifred Gérin
BROWNING: John Bryson
E. B. BROWNING: Alethea Hayter
SAMUEL BUTLER: G. D. H. Cole
BYRON: I, II & III: Bernard Blackstone
CARLYLE: David Gascoyne
LEWIS CARROLL: Derek Hudson
COLERIDGE: Kathleen Raine
CREEVEY & GREVILLE: J. Richardson
DE QUINCEY: Hugh Sykes Davies
DICKENS: K. J. Fielding
    EARLY NOVELS: T. Blount
    LATER NOVELS: B. Hardy
DISRAELI: Paul Bloomfield
GEORGE ELIOT: Lettice Cooper
FERRIER & GALT: W. M. Parker
FITZGERALD: Joanna Richardson
ELIZABETH GASKELL: Miriam Allott
GISSING: A. C. Ward
THOMAS HARDY: R. A. Scott-James
    and C. Day Lewis
HAZLITT: J. B. Priestley
HOOD: Laurence Brander
G. M. HOPKINS: Geoffrey Grigson
T. H. HUXLEY: William Irvine
KEATS: Edmund Blunden
LAMB: Edmund Blunden
LANDOR: G. Rostrevor Hamilton
EDWARD LEAR: Joanna Richardson
MACAULAY: G. R. Potter
MEREDITH: Phyllis Bartlett
JOHN STUART MILL: M. Cranston
WILLIAM MORRIS: P. Henderson
NEWMAN: J. M. Cameron
PATER: Ian Fletcher
PEACOCK: J. I. M. Stewart
ROSSETTI: Oswald Doughty
CHRISTINA ROSSETTI: G. Battiscombe
RUSKIN: Peter Quennell
SIR WALTER SCOTT: Ian Jack
SHELLEY: G. M. Matthews
SOUTHEY: Geoffrey Carnall
LESLIE STEPHEN: Phyllis Grosskurth
R. L. STEVENSON: G. B. Stern

SWINBURNE: Ian Fletcher
TENNYSON: B. C. Southam
THACKERAY: Laurence Brander
FRANCIS THOMPSON: P. Butter
TROLLOPE: Hugh Sykes Davies
OSCAR WILDE: James Laver
WORDSWORTH: Helen Darbishire

Twentieth Century:

CHINUA ACHEBE: A. Ravenscroft
W. H. AUDEN: Richard Hoggart
SAMUEL BECKETT: J-J. Mayoux
HILAIRE BELLOC: Renée Haynes
ARNOLD BENNETT: F. Swinnerton
EDMUND BLUNDEN: Alec M. Har
ROBERT BRIDGES: J. Sparrow
ANTHONY BURGESS: Carol M.]
ROY CAMPBELL: David Wright
JOYCE CAREY: Walter Allen
G. K. CHESTERTON: C. Hollis
WINSTON CHURCHILL: John Con:
R. G. COLLINGWOOD: E. W. F. Ton
I. COMPTON-BURNETT:
                R. Glynn Gr
JOSEPH CONRAD: Oliver Warner
WALTER DE LA MARE: K. Hopl
NORMAN DOUGLAS: Ian Greenle
LAWRENCE DURRELL: G. S. Fra
T. S. ELIOT: M. C. Bradbrook
T. S. ELIOT: The Making of
   'The Waste Land': M. C. Bradbr(
FORD MADOX FORD: Kenneth Yo
E. M. FORSTER: Rex Warner
CHRISTOPHER FRY: Derek Stanfo
JOHN GALSWORTHY: R. H. Mott
ROBERT GRAVES: M. Seymour-Sn
GRAHAM GREENE: Francis Wyndh
L. P. HARTLEY: Paul Bloomfield
A. E. HOUSMAN: Ian Scott-Kilver
TED HUGHES: Keith Sagar
ALDOUS HUXLEY: Jocelyn Brook(
HENRY JAMES: Michael Swan
PAMELA HANSFORD JOHNSON:
                Isabel Qu
JAMES JOYCE: J. I. M. Stewart
RUDYARD KIPLING: Bonamy Dol
D. H. LAWRENCE: Kenneth Your
DORIS LESSING: Michael Thorpe
C. DAY LEWIS: Clifford Dyment
WYNDHAM LEWIS: E. W. F. Ton
COMPTON MACKENZIE: K. Your
LOUIS MACNEICE: John Press
KATHERINE MANSFIELD: Ian Gor